ANNEMARIE MEINTJES
& KAREN ROOS

PHOTOGRAPHY BY

MASSIMO CECCONI

FAST

COR

C O N T E N T S

C O N T E N T S

This is a book of clever decorating tricks that will instantly brighten up your home. Some of these ideas are our own, while others we've picked up over the years photographing homes for magazines.

In the pages that follow, you'll find ideas on how to dress a naked light bulb while searching for the perfect chandelier, or how to display the family photo album without spending your inheritance on frames. You'll also discover the everyday magic of tea lights and the use of fairy lights beyond the Christmas tree. It's window-dressing rather than curtain making; creating

ABOUT THIS BOOK

accents with colour, using objects from nature and learning to rethink, recycle and revamp before you go out and spend money.

All in all it's about styling up your home for a party, a special guest's visit or for a photographic shoot. The best part is that it looks great and costs little enough to enable you to restyle it as often as you wish.

Annemarie Meintjes and Karen Roos

ONE

RETHINK

rethink *vb.* to think again about something (a plan, idea or system) in order to change or improve it

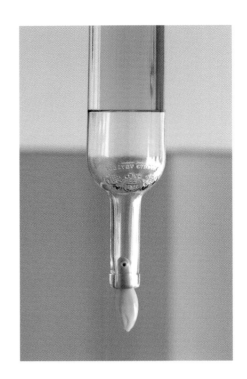

LOOK BEYOND THE ORIGINAL FUNCTION

IF THE SHAPE OF A CONTAINER PLEASES YOU, REMOVE THE BRANDING AND RECYCLE IT INTO

A CITRONELLA LANTERN, A VASE OR A DECANTER.

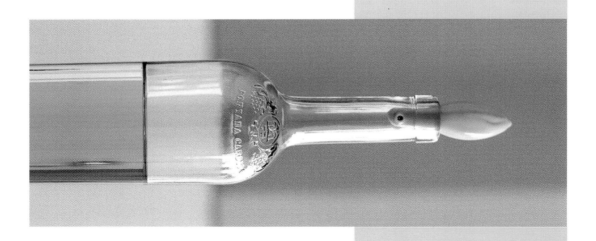

DE-BOXED

IF YOU THINK BOXED WINE IS NOT YOUR THING, THEN THINK AGAIN. ONCE EMPTY, THE BAG IN THE BOX TRANSFORMS INTO THE IDEAL SHAMPOO/BODY WASH DISPENSER FOR THE SHOWER. REMOVE THE BOX, RINSE AND IT'S READY TO GO. DE-BOXED, THE BAGS ALSO MAKE FUNKY SCATTER CUSHIONS WHEN INFLATED OR FILLED WITH POLYSTYRENE BALLS, SHREDDED PAPER OR PLASTIC.

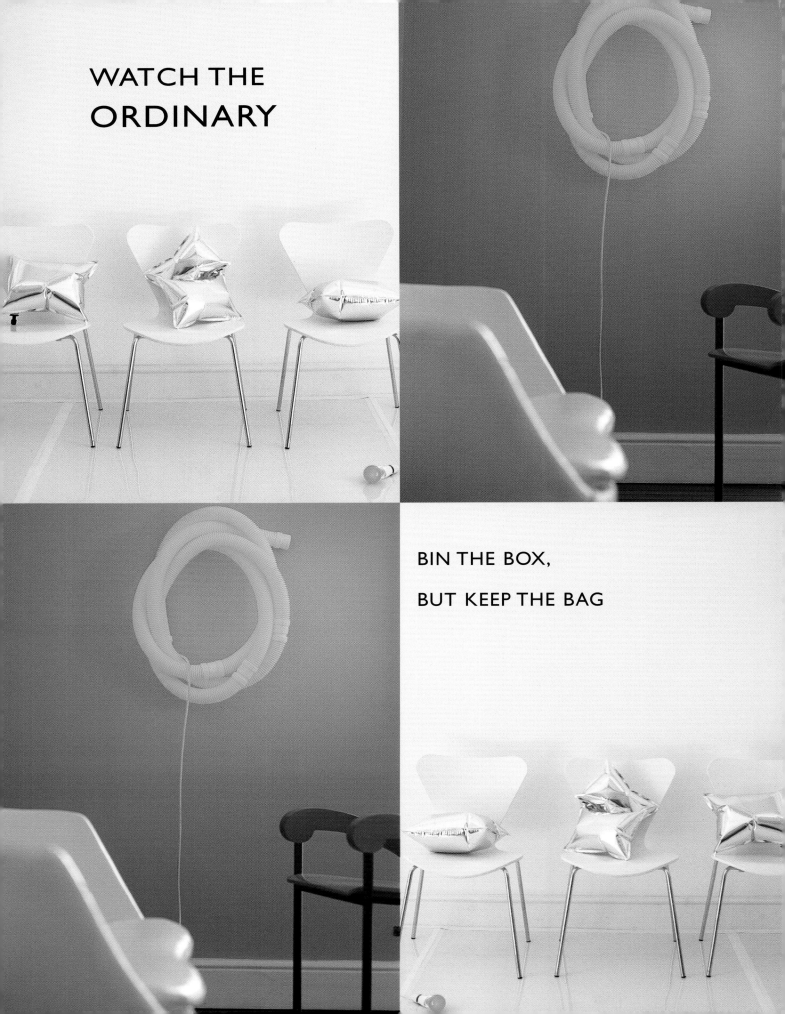

WATCH THE
ORDINARY

BIN THE BOX,
BUT KEEP THE BAG

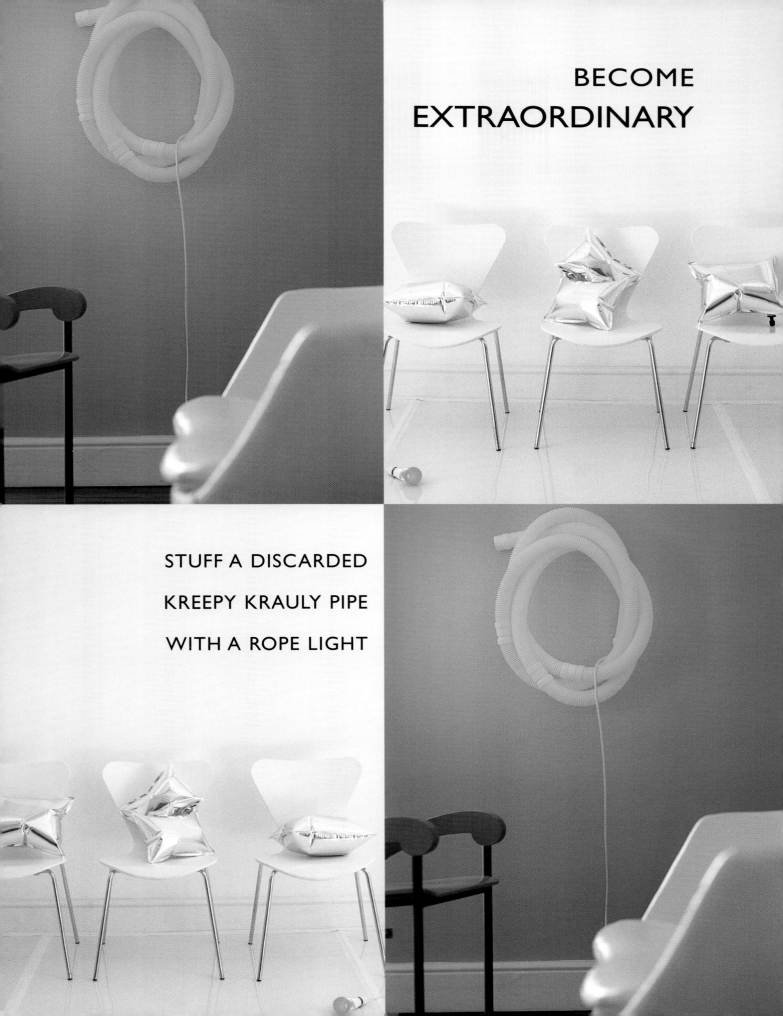

BECOME
EXTRAORDINARY

STUFF A DISCARDED

KREEPY KRAULY PIPE

WITH A ROPE LIGHT

RESCUE YOUR ROOM FROM A SHY AND RETIRING WALL FINISH

TO CREATE AN INSTANT AND SPECTACULAR WALL FINISH WITH A WONDERFUL IRIDESCENT GLOW, STICK POLYSTYRENE APPLE TRAYS AGAINST THE WALL, USING THE SILVER-GREEN FLIPSIDE ON THE OUTSIDE. LIGHT AS A FEATHER, THE TRAYS WILL STAY UP AGAINST THE WALL WITH TINY PIECES OF PRESTIK BUT, IF YOU PLAN TO KEEP THEM UP FOR A LONG PERIOD, THEN STICK THEM ON WITH DOUBLE-SIDED VELCRO SQUARES, WHICH WILL ALLOW YOU TO TAKE THEM DOWN FOR CLEANING.

APPLE TRAYS MEASURE 36 CM X 58 CM, SO YOU CAN WORK OUT HOW MANY YOU NEED AND RETRIEVE THEM FROM SUPERMARKET DEPOTS OR TEAM UP WITH FRIENDS TO ORDER A STASH DIRECTLY FROM THE SUPPLIER. THEY'RE GREAT FOR LOFTS, OFFICES AND EVEN KIDS' ROOMS AND STUDENTS' DIGS.

REINVENT EVERYDAY OBJECTS

AIRLINE-STYLE MEAL TRAYS HAVE BECOME THE ULTIMATE TABLEWARE FOR TREND-AWARE URBANITES. SHOP IN ARMY SURPLUS STORES FOR STAINLESS-STEEL VERSIONS.

ONE SHEET OF BUBBLE FOIL CEILING INSULATION PIERCED WITH THE GLOBES FROM A STRING OF FAIRY LIGHTS CREATES A TALKING POINT – ON A WALL OR AS A ROOM DIVIDER. FOR KIDS' ROOMS, BACK IT WITH ANOTHER SHEET AND SEAL THE SIDES TO CONTAIN THE FAIRY LIGHTS.

LATERAL THINKING =
CREATIVE SPACES

LOVE AT FIRST LIGHT

TOO OFTEN THE MOST BEAUTIFUL ROOMS DECORATED WITH THE GREATEST OF CARE SHARE A COMMON TROUBLE SPOT – THE NAKED LIGHT BULB.

BUY THE BIGGEST LIGHT BULB YOU CAN FIND AND GO BARE, OR LOOK AROUND YOU FOR ORDINARY, UNEXPECTED ITEMS THAT CAN BE TURNED INTO LAMPSHADES. DRESS A BULB IN A HUMBLE FISHING BASKET AND CREATE A WORK OF ART.

FAST-TRACK
LIGHTING

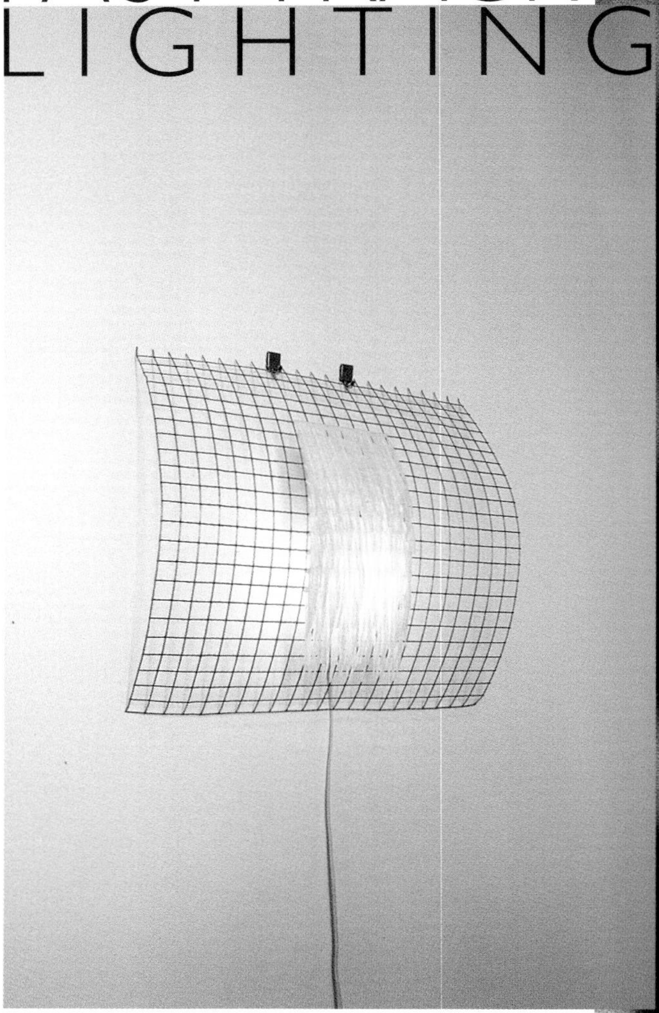

DRESS LIGHTS

CREATE A WALL LIGHT WITH METAL

MESH FENCING AND CABLE TIES

(DESIGNED TO TIE ELECTRICAL CABLES

TOGETHER AND ALSO USED BY

AIRPORT ATTENDANTS TO SEAL ZIPPER

BAGS). ALTERNATIVELY, YOU CAN STRIP

AN OLD LAMPSHADE AND TIE THE TAGS

TO THE FRAME.

MAKE LIGHT WORK OF IT

POLYPROPYLENE SHEETING IS SOLD BY THE METRE AND,

ONCE CUT, CURLS UP NATURALLY INTO A ROLL. SIMPLY

PLACE A LOW VOLTAGE LIGHT SOURCE IN THE CENTRE

OF THE ROLL TO MAKE A CYLINDRICAL LAMP.

ROLL PLAYING

DUMP THE
DOCUMENTS
AND STORE WINE
IN TUBES.

CUT TUBES MANUFACTURED FOR THE CARPET INDUSTRY TO SIZE AND TOP WITH A SHEET OF SANDBLASTED GLASS TO MAKE A GREAT TABLE.

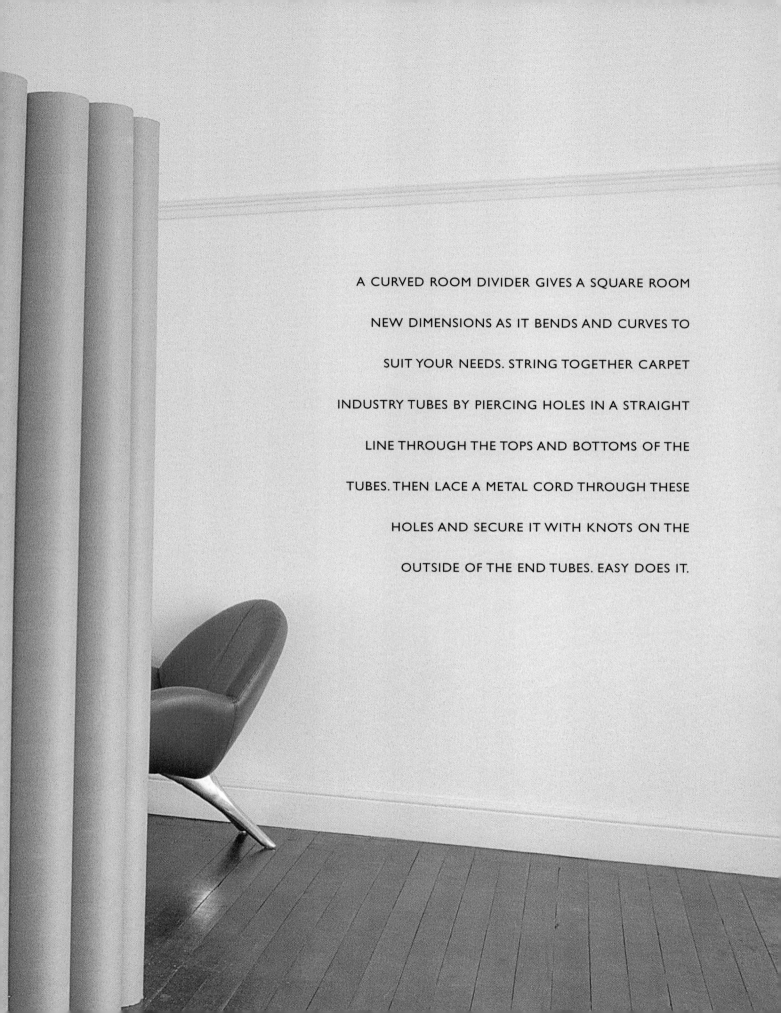

A CURVED ROOM DIVIDER GIVES A SQUARE ROOM
NEW DIMENSIONS AS IT BENDS AND CURVES TO
SUIT YOUR NEEDS. STRING TOGETHER CARPET
INDUSTRY TUBES BY PIERCING HOLES IN A STRAIGHT
LINE THROUGH THE TOPS AND BOTTOMS OF THE
TUBES. THEN LACE A METAL CORD THROUGH THESE
HOLES AND SECURE IT WITH KNOTS ON THE
OUTSIDE OF THE END TUBES. EASY DOES IT.

Ho il profumo
dei tuoi
passi dau
il cuore

TWO
PAPER

paper *n.* a substance made from cellulose fibres derived from rags, wood etc., and formed into flat thin sheets suitable for writing on, decorating walls, wrapping, etc.

paper over *vb.* (*tr. adv.*) to conceal (something controversial or unpleasant)

WINDOW-DRESSING

SEE PAPER AS A

FIBRE. BUY IT BY THE

METRE AND FLAUNT IT.

IT'S THE INSTANT SOLUTION

FOR ROUND WINDOWS.

LIGHT IS LIFE

DRESS A WINDOW IN A

FLURRY OF POST-IT NOTES

SO YOU KEEP THE LIGHT

BUT BLOCK OUT

UNSAVOURY VIEWS.

PEG AND PAPER

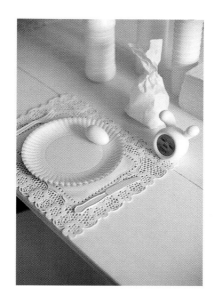

ABOVE: SETTING A TABLE WITH PAPER CAN BE GRAND.

LEFT: BUY A PRINTED GRAPHIC IMAGE, THEN PEG IT, UNFRAMED, ONTO A WALL WITH VELCRO SQUARES FOR AN UNSTRUCTURED LOOK THAT GIVES YOU THE FREEDOM TO CHANGE THE IMAGE TO SUIT YOUR MOOD.

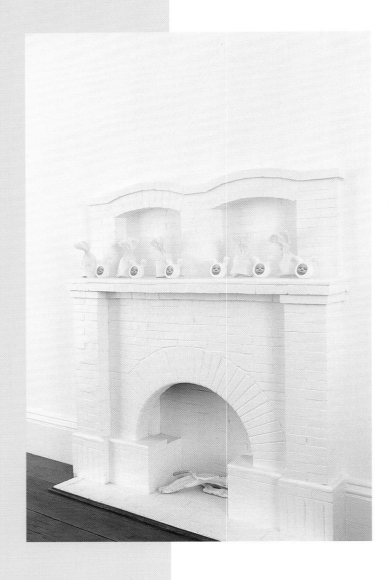

LUXURIATE IN A PAPER ROOM OF YOUR OWN

MAKING ... AS INSPIRED BY LIGHTING GURU INGO

MAURER'S 'ZETTEL'Z'.

PAPER CHANDELIER – GIVE YOUR DOODLES WINGS

FLIGHT
OF FANCY

CREATE A ROMANTIC MOOD WITH THE WELL-THUMBED

PAGES OF A LOVE STORY, INTERSPERSED WITH LOVE

NOTES AND POEMS.

DUFAYLITE IS A LIGHTWEIGHT, FLEXIBLE HONEYCOMB CARDBOARD MATERIAL THAT IS USED COMMERCIALLY TO FILL DOORS. WHEN STRETCHED TO ITS LIMITS IT BECOMES A DESIGNER ROOM DIVIDER.

A LIGHT DRESSER

DUFAYLITE HAS THE RIGHT WEIGHT, THE RIGHT TEXTURE AND THE RIGHT

DELICATE, LACY LOOK. STRETCH IT OUT AND IT CONCERTINAS BACK.

IT CONCEALS AND ALSO REVEALS. IT CAN TRANFORM ITSELF INTO

ANYTHING, EVEN A DRESS! IT IS SOLD PER KILOGRAM, IN ROLLS

OR IN PIECES, AND CAN BE ORDERED TO SIZE.

colour *n.* a substance, such as
dye or paint, that imparts colour

colouring *n.* a false or
misleading appearance

CHARGE
YOUR HOUSE
WITH COLOUR

TWO-TONE TANGO

TAKE ONE COLOUR AND LAYER IT

TONE UPON TONE.

QUICK COLOUR FIX

USE COLOUR AS AN ACCENT TO
BRIGHTEN UP YOUR SPACE. BUY A
BOX OF THE SAME COLOUR FRUIT
OR THE EVER-FRESH PAPER VERSION.
TRAWL THE DEPTHS OF YOUR
LOCAL FISHERMAN'S SUPPLY STORE
FOR GREAT BOTTLE STOPPERS.

BUY COLOUR BY THE METRE OR DYE
IT IN LOADS!

REINVENT OLD STALWARTS WITH DYE AND REVEL IN

THE FACT THAT NO TWO ITEMS IN THE SAME LOAD WILL

BE THE SAME SHADE BECAUSE OF THE ORIGINAL

COLOUR AND FABRIC MIX. YOU CAN OPT FOR DIY IF IT'S

A SMALL BUNDLE IN COTTON, LINEN OR SILK. IF IT'S A

MIXED LOAD, LEAVE IT TO THE PROFESSIONALS.

LUCKY **DIP**

CREATE YOUR OWN ROOM RECIPE

CHANGE THE COLOUR OF A ROOM BY PLAYING WITH COLOURED GLOBES, UPLIGHTERS,

DOWNLIGHTERS, SPOTS … THE POSSIBILITIES ARE ENDLESS.

SUPER-FAST DÉCOR

DISPLAY EVERYTHING IN THE SAME COLOUR AND

STORE THE REST!

PLAY WITH STRIPES

INSTANT WALLPAPER: HANG STRIPS OF COLOURED

PLASTIC AT REGULAR INTERVALS ON THE WALLS. GLUE OR

STAPLE THE STRIPS TO THE PICTURE RAIL (OR CORNICE)

AND SKIRTING BOARDS.

PLAY WITH SPRAY PAINT

IGNORE MATT PAINTS, SHINE IS THE NEW THING. DON'T

WASTE TIME WITH REGULAR SPRAY PAINT, BUT GO FOR

METALLIC AUTO SPRAY PAINT WITH AN EXCITING RANGE

OF COLOURS THAT DRY HARD AND FAST.

COOL COLOURS – CLEVER WALLS

PAINT UPDATES, RENEWS AND EXCITES. TAKE IT BEYOND THE

WALLS TO WOOD STAINS AND METALLIC PAINTS.

THE FACT THAT YOU CAN TAKE A FASHION ITEM TO ALMOST

ANY HARDWARE STORE AND HAVE PAINT MIXED IN THE EXACT

SHADE IS WHY DECORATORS LOVE TO PAINT. THE FACT THAT

YOU CAN REPAINT IF YOU FIND YOU CAN'T LIVE WITH THE

COLOUR AFTER A WHILE IS WHY THEIR CLIENTS LOVE TO LIVE

OUT THEIR COLOUR FANTASIES.

DON'T BE SHOCKED – PERHAPS YOU SHOULD TRY A BLACK

ROOM NEXT.

FOUR

NATURE

nature *n.* (often cap.) the whole system of the existence, forces and events of all physical life that are not controlled by mankind

natural *adj.* of, existing in, or produced by nature

MAKE NATURE'S CALENDAR OUT OF A POCKET CURTAIN, THEN CHART THE SEASONS FROM FEATHERS TO LEAVES TO FLOWERS TO HOLLY.

STYLE ON A STRING

SEASONAL SOUVENIRS OR COUNTRY CUTTINGS

ADD AN AIR OF SPIRITUAL FREEDOM TO A SIMPLE

STRING CURTAIN. TIE STRINGS TO A FALLEN

BRANCH OR A PIECE OF DRIFTWOOD AND

REMEMBER TO TIE THE HEAVIER OBJECTS

TO THE LOWER ENDS OF EACH LENGTH TO

WEIGH THEM DOWN.

TACTILE TOUCHES TO MAKE YOU PURR

ADORN A ROUND SCATTER CUSHION OR BARSTOOL
WITH SUPER-SOFT WHITE OSTRICH FEATHERS.
DISPLAY YOUR STASH OF PORCUPINE QUILLS IN
AN ORIGINAL WAY.

DARE TO BE
DIFFERENT

THE SECRET HISTORY ...

... OF A WEATHERED SHELL GIVES AN
OVAL MIRROR A ROMANTIC PAST.

BEAUTY BRANCHES OUT

DEAD BRANCHES HAVE BEAUTY – TAKE THEM INTO YOUR HOME AND

USE THEM AS CENTREPIECES ABOVE THE TABLE OR TURN THEM INTO

CHANDELIERS USING FAIRY LIGHTS OR HANGING TEA LIGHTS.

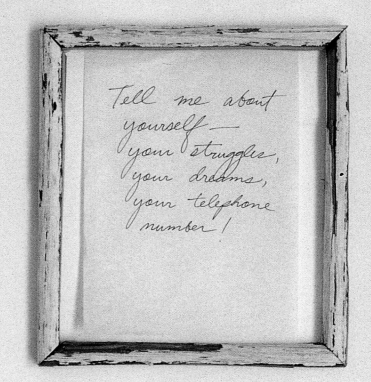

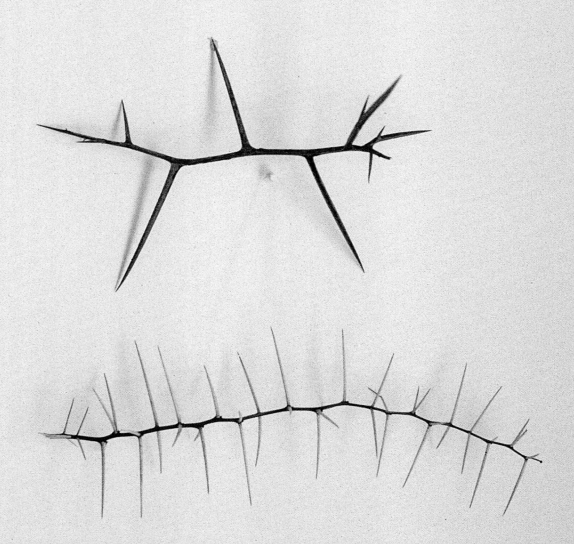

BARK AS BIRD IN FLIGHT

ORGANICS ARE THE HEARTBEAT OF DESIGN. A PIECE

OF BARK GIVES MOVEMENT TO A STATIC WALL.

TREE TRUNKS AS TABLES

SAVE THE TREE TRUNKS! AND RECYCLE INTO

ROBUST SIDE TABLES.

COME BACK SLEEPERS

IN THE CURRENT MOOD OF ECO-AWARENESS, TEXTURES AND

SCULPTURAL FORMS LEAD THE WAY, MAKING THE RAILWAY SLEEPER THE

LOOK OF THE MOMENT. IT'S AN UNTREATED, WEATHERED, LAYERED AND

ORGANIC FEEL THAT IS ENHANCED BY THE SHAPES THAT SURROUND IT.

STRAW MATTRESSES OR CRISP LINEN COMPLIMENTS SLEEPERS AND

CREATES A FEELING OF SANCTUARY. KEEP THEM NATURAL AND TURN

THEM INTO A BED, A DAY BED OR EVEN A SUN BED ON THE DECK.

PURITY IS KEY.

FIVE

PHOTOGRAPHS

photographs *n.* images of an object, person, scene, etc., in the form of a print or slide recorded by camera

photostat *n.* 1. *Trademark.* a machine or process used to make photographic copies of written, printed or graphic matter 2. any copy made by such a machine

YOU HAVE BEEN
FRAMED

FRAMING CAN BE PRICEY. CLEAR CLIPBOARDS AND A4 SHEETS OF ACETATE OFFER AN INEXPENSIVE SOLUTION. ALTERNATIVELY, PHOTOSTAT THE IMAGES ONTO ARCHITECT'S FILM OR A4 SHEETS OF ACETATE. BOLD GRAPHIC IMAGES LOOK GREAT AS ROOM DIVIDERS OR WINDOW BLINDS WHERE YOU WANT TO RETAIN THE LIGHT WITHOUT REVEALING THE VIEW.

LAID BACK LOUNGING WITH A FAMILY FOCUS

USING PHOTOGRAPHS OR PHOTOSTAT IMAGES TO DECORATE YOUR HOME IS A UNIQUE WAY OF PERSONALISING YOUR

SPACE. IT ALSO PROVIDES UNUSUAL SURFACES FOR DISPLAYING THE FAMILY ALBUM. PHOTOSTATS ARE INEXPENSIVE AND

VARY FROM A5 SIZE TO THE CLASSIC A0 POSTER SIZE. IT CAN BE DONE ON ANY COLOUR PAPER, ACETATE, ARCHITECT'S

FILM, FABRIC AND EVEN ON CROCKERY.

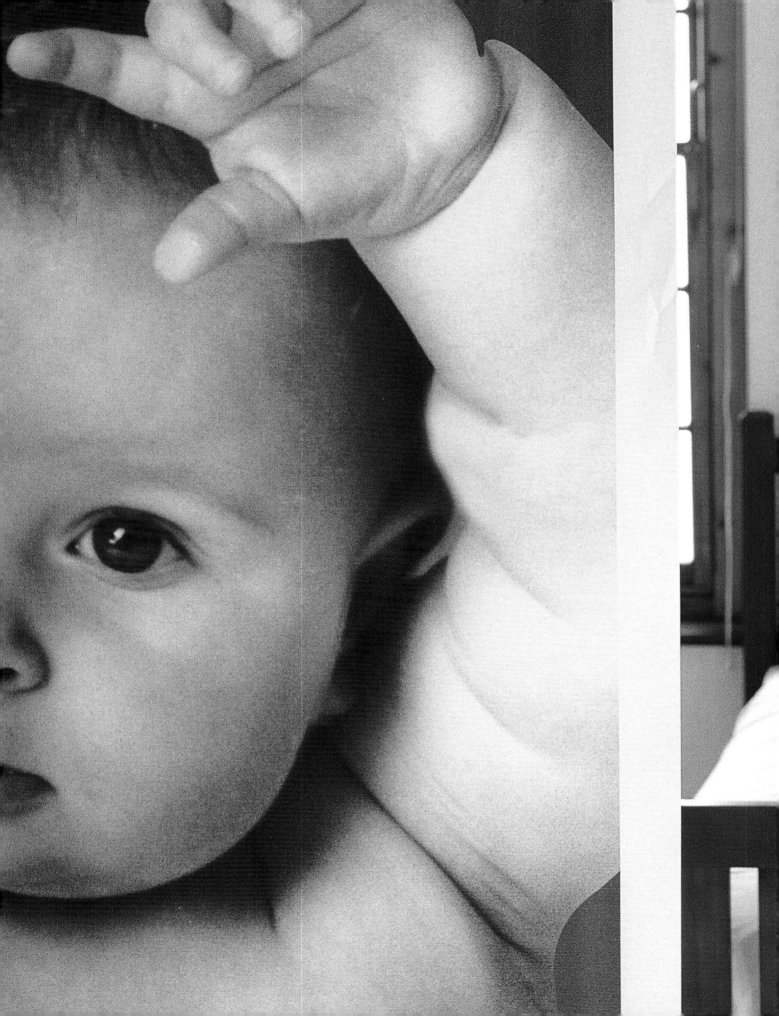

BLOW UP YOUR FAVOURITE BABY

PHOTOGRAPH AND TURN IT INTO

A ROOM DIVIDER. COPY THE SAME

IMAGE ONTO BED LINEN –

ANDY WARHOL STYLE.

SKIN DEEP

SPECIAL PHOTOGRAPHS SHOULD GET THE BIG TREATMENT –

HAVE THEM PRINTED ONTO CANVAS AND BE SURE TO SEAL THE

IMAGE IF YOU INTEND TO USE IT IN THE BATHROOM.

CONCERTINA COLLAGE

THIS COLLAGE OF FAMILY PHOTOGRAPHS AND MEMORIES

MAKES AN INTERESTING ALTERNATIVE TO A CLUSTER OF

BITTY FRAMES.

MIRROR, MIRROR ...

TAKE THE EDGE OFF AN IMPOSING MIRROR BY LAYERING IT

WITH HOLIDAY SNAPS. SUCTION HOOKS AND CABLE

SYSTEMS ALLOW YOU TO USE YOUR MIRROR AS A PINBOARD.

ABOVE: WE ALL GATHER IMAGES AND PHOTOGRAPHS THAT

WE LOVE. CAPTURE YOURS BY PRINTING THEM ONTO PLACE

MATS. DO IT ON A3 BROWN PAPER AND DISCARD AFTER THE

MEAL OR LAMINATE IT FOR POSTERITY.

LEFT: USE SIMPLE GRAPHIC IMAGES FOR A POWERFUL EFFECT.

PICTURE THIS

SNOW GLOBES ARE FUN AND CLEVER CONVERSATION OPENERS. THEY LOOK

JUST AS GOOD ON THE MANTELPIECE AS THEY DO NEXT TO THE IMAC. USE

THEM AT A DINNER PARTY TO INDICATE PLACE SETTINGS WITH PHOTO

IMAGES INSTEAD OF NAMES. SNOW GLOBES ARE DESIGNED IN SUCH A

WAY THAT PHOTOGRAPHS OR MESSSAGES CAN BE SLIPPED INTO THE

GLOBE FROM THE BASE BY TURNING THE GLOBE UPSIDE DOWN AND

REMOUNTING THE DISC. INSERT PHOTOGRAPHS OR MESSAGES ON BOTH

SIDES OF THE DISC AND REPLACE.

SIX

TEA LIGHTS

light *n.* anything that illuminates,
such as a lamp or candle

light up *vb.* (*adv.*) to make or
become cheerful or animated

ABOVE: TURN ANY GLASS JARS INTO LANTERNS AND CLUSTER TOGETHER FOR IMPACT.

RIGHT: SPRINKLE GLITTER ON A SHEET OF PAPER, PAINT THE TEA LIGHT'S METAL CASING WITH A COAT OF PVA CRAFT GLUE AND ROLL IN GLITTER.

LINE UP TEA LIGHTS IN DISPOSABLE COLOURED

GLASSES. CHOOSE A COLOUR TO SUIT YOUR

MOOD AND CHANGE THE COLOUR AS YOU

CHANGE YOUR MOOD.

FIRE LIGHT, FIRE BRIGHT

TEA LIGHTS ARE INEXPENSIVE, INDEPENDENT AND INDISPENSABLE IN TODAY'S HOME. THESE LITTLE CANDLES CAN STAND ON THEIR OWN OR GIVE THEIR MAGIC GLOW TO ANY HOLDER WHEN POPPED INSIDE ONE. REMEMBER, IT'S STILL A CANDLE WITH A FLAME, SO IT'S BEST NOT LEFT ALONE AND SHOULD ONLY BURN IN COMPANY.

FILL HOT DOG BAGS WITH WHITE RIVER SAND TO ANCHOR THEM, THEN PLACE THE TEA LIGHT IN THE CENTRE TO AVOID THE BAGS CATCHING FIRE.

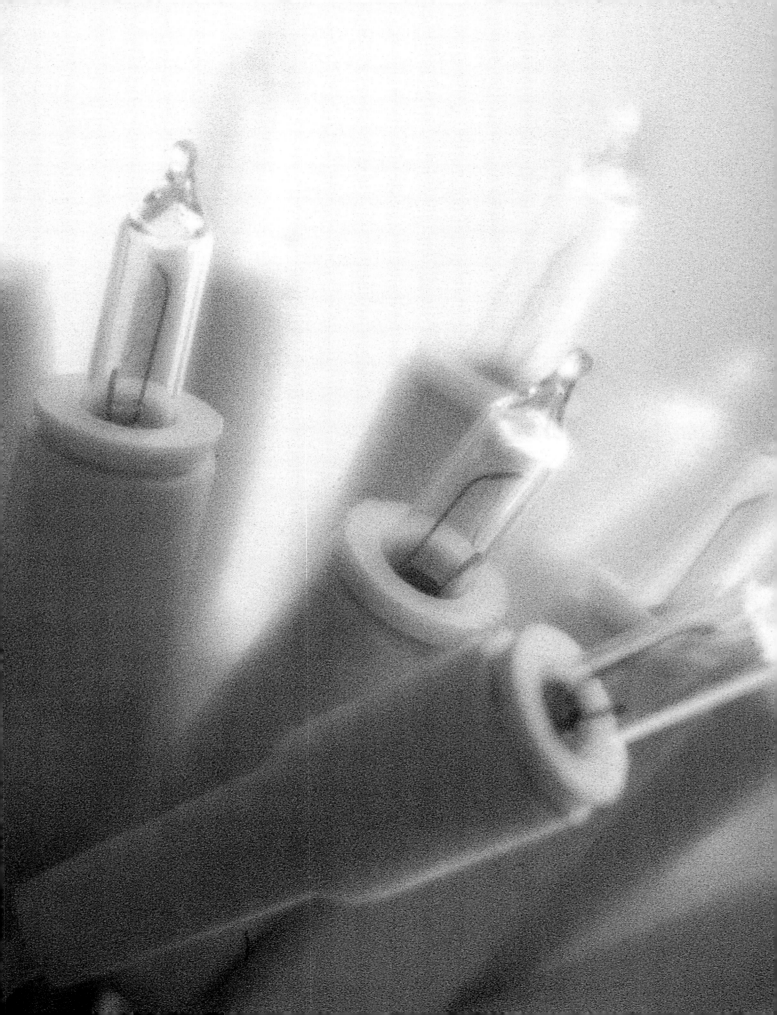

SEVEN

FAIRY LIGHTS

fairy lights *pl. n.* small coloured electric bulbs strung together and used for decoration, esp. on a Christmas tree

fairyland *n.* a fantasy world, esp. one resulting from a person's wild imaginings

TO MAKE A CANISTER LIGHT, SIMPLY

PUNCH A HOLE INTO THE LID OF AN

EMPTY FILM CONTAINER AND PUSH THE

FAIRY GLOBE THROUGH. YOU NEED ONE

CANISTER PER GLOBE, SO START SAVING

NOW OR COLLECT THE REST FROM YOUR

NEAREST FILM-PROCESSING LAB.

CONTAINED

MAGIC

THIS PAGE: FILL ANY DISCARDED *OBJET* WITH FAIRY

LIGHTS AND IT BECOMES A DESIRED *OBJET*.

RIGHT: A HONEYCOMB LIGHT WORKS WELL AS

A ROOM DIVIDER.

PAPER LANTERNS

USE A STANLEY KNIFE TO CUT A CROSS INTO THE BASES

OF TINY COOKIE CUPS. PUSH THROUGH THE BULB OF A

FAIRY LIGHT TO MAKE A PAPER LANTERN, THEN DRAPE IT

AROUND A MIRROR OR ABOVE THE BED.

MAGIC IN FAIRYLAND

CREATE YOUR OWN MAGICAL ARTWORK: SIMPLY PUNCH HOLES IN

A CLEAN CANVAS AND PUSH FAIRY LIGHT BULBS THROUGH. IT'S A

GOOD IDEA TO LEAVE THE LIGHTS ON WHEN PUSHING THEM

THROUGH TO ENSURE THAT THE CONNECTIONS ARE INTACT. FAIRY

LIGHTS HAVE A LOW VOLTAGE AND ARE HARMLESS.

LIGHT LINE

NEON-LIKE ROPE LIGHTS ARE SOLD PER METRE AND CAN BE INSTALLED ANYWHERE WITH SILICONE GLUE. UNLIKE NEON LIGHTS THE ROPE LIGHT IS FLEXIBLE: YOU CAN BEND IT, CUT IT, CONNECT SEVERAL LENGTHS TOGETHER AND MOULD IT INTO ANY SHAPE YOU LIKE. THEY'RE GREAT FOR STAIRCASES AND DARK PASSAGES AND YOU CAN EVEN TAKE THEM RIGHT AROUND THE ROOM ON SKIRTING BOARDS FOR A COSY GLOW. ALTERNATIVELY YOU CAN SPIRAL A BLUE ROPE LIGHT ABOVE YOUR BED TO MATCH YOUR MOOD. THE POSSIBILITIES ARE ENDLESS!

This book is not meant to motivate you to spend money or send you on a

shopping spree. It was written to inspire you and to make you look at everyday

objects with different eyes.

Most of the items used to illustrate the ideas were designed as packaging,

which was collected or rescued from garbage cans. We've often stumbled across

items in hardware and speciality stores that inspired us to come up with new

ideas, but these items are basic and available countrywide.

Impatient decorators who cannot wait until they've collected their own

resources can try contacting manufacturers direct. Please keep in mind that some

companies do not supply directly to the public, or require minimum orders, but

they will direct you to a stockist in your area. Alternatively, ask to purchase

reject material. The product may have been rejected for the purpose it was

designed for because of a slight imperfection, but for décor purposes it is perfect.

ACKNOWLEDGEMENTS

THANK YOU!

To **Ingo Maurer,** whose 'Zettel'z' chandelier was the inspiration for chapter two. Don't you just love his 'Lucellino' with goose feather wings on pages 38 and 39? See also page 75 where we framed one of the notes from the 'Zettel'z' chandelier.

To **Elliott Erwitt,** whose dog postcards appear on pages 82 and 91. His boxed postcard collection called DogDOGS is available from Exclusive Books.

To **Stephen Inggs,** for the use of his artwork on pages 34, 37, 84, 92 and 107. If you love them, you can own them! Contact him on 00 27 (0) 21 434 7581.

To **Dook,** for the use of 'Nikki' on page 89 from his book *Skin and Bone*. Books and prints available from Dook on 00 27 (0) 11 726 3568.

To **Michael Methven,** for the use of his papier-mâché buffalo light fitting on page 71. To commission him for animal head light fittings, contact him at The Pan African Market Gallery on 00 27 (0) 21 424 2957.

To **Lindi Sales,** for the use of her family collage on page 90. To commission her for a personlized family collage phone her on 00 27 (0) 21 689 1873.

To **Francesco Sardella,** for the use of his photograph of dogs on page 83.

To **Annel Botha,** for the use of baby Elke Hansen's photograph on pages 80, 86 and 87.

To **Sonja Zimberlin,** for the use of her painting on page 52. To commission her for a bold and colourful canvas, phone her on 00 27 (0) 21 423 3540.

To **Russel Jones** from Scan Shop, for scans and prints for chapter five.

To **Rosalind Stone**, public relations officer for Kohler, for introducing us to their wonderful products.

This edition first published in 2002 by
New Holland Publishers (UK) Ltd
Garfield House
86–88 Edgware Road
London W2 2EA
United Kingdom
www.newhollandpublishers.com

10 9 8 7 6 5 4 3 2 1

Editor: Joy Clack
Copy editor: Kerryn du Preez
Designer: Petal Palmer
Design assistant: Natascha Adendorff
Photographer: Massimo Cecconi
Photographic assistant: Francesco Sardella
Production assistant: Alison Faure

Reproduction by Hirt & Carter Cape (Pty) Ltd
Printed and bound by Sing Cheong Printing Company Limited

ISBN 1 84330 356 6